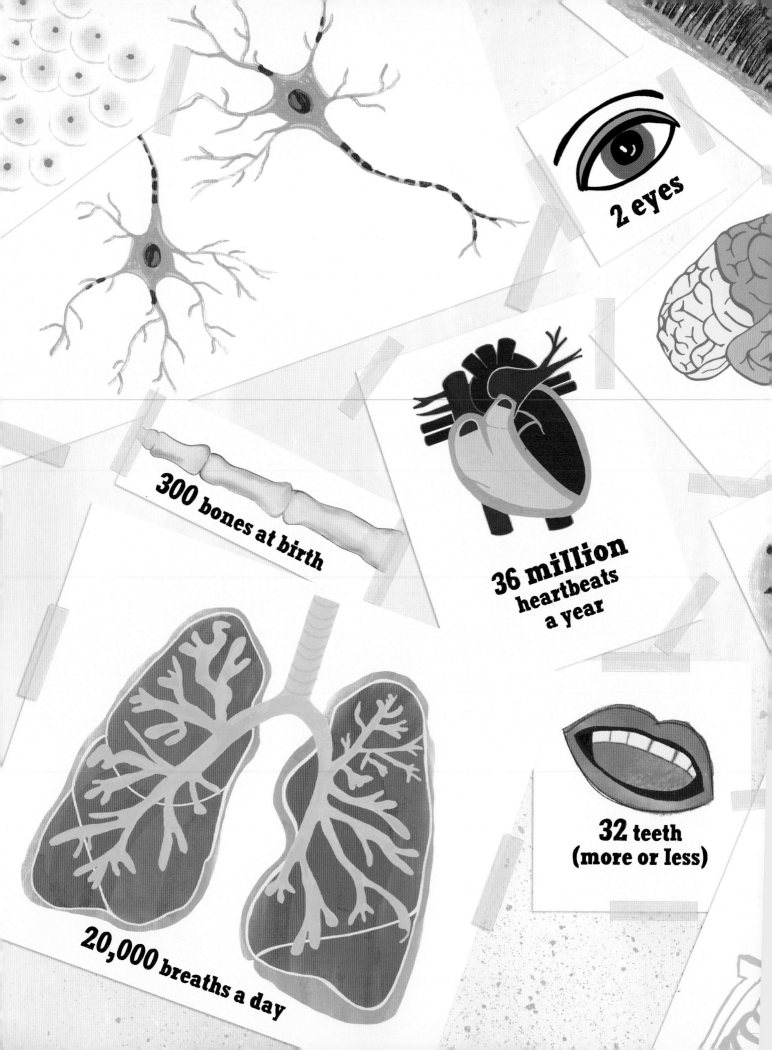

2 eyes

300 bones at birth

36 million heartbeats a year

32 teeth (more or less)

20,000 breaths a day

NUMBER TOURS for CURIOUS KIDS

A Tour of the HUMAN BODY

Amazing Numbers– Fantastic Facts

What are you made of?
How does your body work?
Come on our tour and see
how numbers tell the amazing tale.

by
JENNIFER BERNE

Illustrated by
DAWN DeVRIES SOKOL

KANE PRESS

AN IMPRINT OF ASTRA BOOKS
FOR YOUNG READERS
New York

To curious minds, number-lovers, and truth-seekers.—*JB*
For Lola—*DDS*

Kane Press
An imprint of Astra Books for Young Readers,
a division of Astra Publishing House
astrapublishinghouse.com
Printed in China

Library of Congress Cataloging-in-Publication Data
Names: Berne, Jennifer, author. | DeVries Sokol, Dawn, illustrator.
Title: A tour of the human body : amazing numbers—fantastic facts / by
  Jennifer Berne ; illustrated by Dawn DeVries Sokol.
Other titles: Amazing numbers-fantastic facts
Description: First edition. | New York : Kane Press, an imprint of Astra
  Books for Young Readers, [2024] | Series: Number tours for curious kids
  | Audience: Ages 5-9 | Audience: Grades 2-3 | Summary: "A tour of the
  body, in which the reader learns about cells, the senses, the stomach,
  bones and muscles, the lungs and heart, and everything that makes the
  body tick. Complete with backmatter and activities"-- Provided by
  publisher.
Identifiers: LCCN 2023026905 (print) | LCCN 2023026906 (ebook) | ISBN
  9781662670152 (hardcover) | ISBN 9781662670169 (ebk)
Subjects: LCSH: Human anatomy--Miscellanea--Juvenile literature. | Human
  body--Miscellanea--Juvenile literature. | Human
  physiology--Miscellanea--Juvenile literature.
Classification: LCC QM27 .B47 2024 (print) | LCC QM27 (ebook) | DDC
  612--dc23/eng/20230907
LC record available at https://lccn.loc.gov/2023026905
LC ebook record available at https://lccn.loc.gov/2023026906

First edition

10 9 8 7 6 5 4 3 2 1

Design by Dawn DeVries Sokol
The text is set in Helvetica regular.
The titles and display type are set in Hand Scribble Sketch regular.
The illustrations are done in Procreate and Photoshop.

You know your height, you know your weight.
And sometimes you even know your temperature.

But there are other numbers—

surprising extraordinary numbers—
that tell the story of you and your body.

A story that starts
right here . . .

Did you know?
Our bodies are made up of over **30 trillion cells.**

Skin cells, muscle cells, nerve cells, bone cells, brain cells . . .
all the little bits of stuff we're built of.

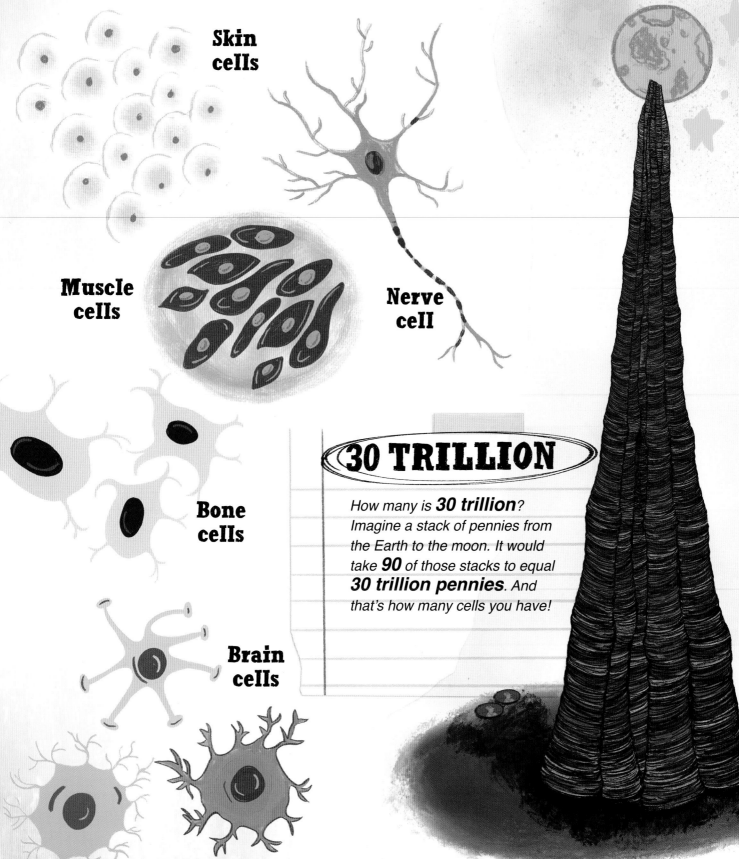

Skin cells

Muscle cells

Nerve cell

Bone cells

Brain cells

30 TRILLION

How many is **30 trillion**?
Imagine a stack of pennies from
the Earth to the moon. It would
take **90** of those stacks to equal
30 trillion pennies. And
that's how many cells you have!

But the body you'll have tomorrow won't
be the same as the body you have today.
That's because our cells are continually replacing themselves.
So you're continually being rebuilt.

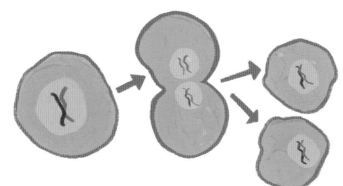

Cells divide to make new cells.

Fresh new stomach cells replace old ones **every few days**,
Our blood cells last up to **4 months**,
Fat cells around **8 years**,
Muscle cells for around **15 years**,
And most brain cells, for **your whole life**.

The entire surface of your skin is replaced every month. That means you will have about **1,000** *new skins in your life!*

Fat cells

Stomach cell

15 million cells in your body were replaced by new ones in the time it took you to read this sentence.

Blood cells

And, speaking of reading, you're doing it with your eyes.

Your amazing eyes

  that can read faster than you can talk

    and see things as small as a speck of dust

  and as far away as the planets and the stars.

Inside your eyes, you have **137 million** light-sensing cells.

  130 million of them let you see in dim light, in shades of gray.

And **7 million** let you see in bright light in color.

137 MILLION

*How many light-sensing cells is **137 million**? Well, that's about the same number as the grains of sugar it would take to fill **157 cups**.*

Your eyes are quite busy.

  They blink around **15 times** each minute . . .

    15,000 times while you're awake each day.

  And, during those waking hours,

    your eyes can focus and refocus about **50 times** per second.

The muscles that help you focus move about **100,000 times** per day.

Focusing is what your eyes do to see things clearly—near things, far things, and everything in between. Our eyes can't do all that at once (try seeing near and far at the same time!), so our eye muscles are always adjusting and readjusting, to make the things we choose to look at clear and not blurry.

COLORS

Here's how talented your eyes are. This chart shows you **hundreds of different colors.** But that's just a tiny fraction of what your eyes are able to see. Most eyes can recognize up to **10 million different colors!**

Next to your busy eyes are your very busy ears.

Ears that start listening before you were born
and keep listening **24** hours a day,
even while you're asleep.
And to do all that listening
your ears have **15,000** hair cells deep inside
that vibrate with incoming sounds—
high sounds, low sounds, loud sounds, and quiet sounds—
telling your brain what's going on all around you.

THUMP!
THUMP!

BALANCE

Ears help you balance too! Your **3** semicircular canals are filled with fluid that helps to detect your position, so you know if you're leaning left or right, lying horizontal, standing upright, or hanging upside-down.

15,000 HAIR CELLS (in Cochlea)

The outside of your ear funnels
sound waves into
your ear canal.

Those waves vibrate your eardrum,
which sends the vibrations
through your ear
to the hair cells
in your cochlea.

Those hairs wiggle
and turn the sounds into
electrical signals that travel
to your brain,
which recognizes the sound.

Semicircular canals

Nerves to Brain

Ear canal

Sound travels into here

Cochlea

Ear drum

Tube to nose/throat

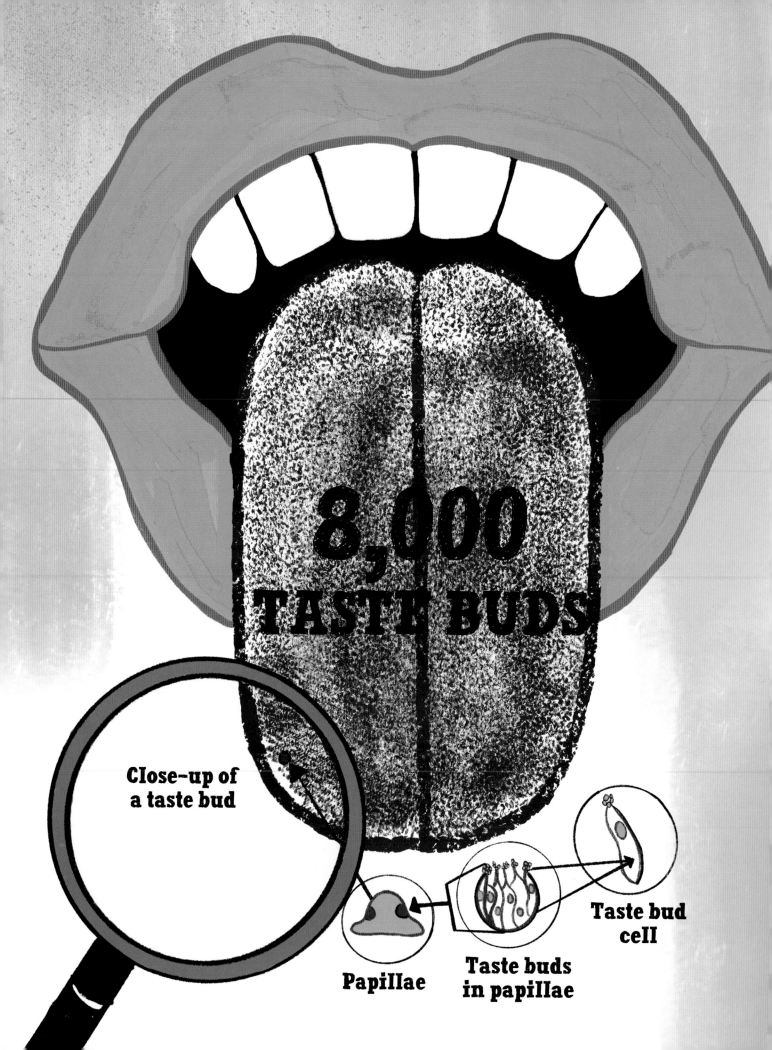

From your ears it's only a few inches down to your mouth.

Inside your mouth you'll find a bit of saliva.

With more and more flowing through all the time.

So much of it in fact that in an average lifetime

you'll produce enough saliva to fill **2** swimming pools.

And then there's your tongue.

It's covered in taste buds.

About **8,000** of them.

But they can only taste **5** flavors:

sweet, salty, sour, bitter, and umami.

(Umami is the richness we love in cheese and meat.)

5 FLAVORS

Sweet

Salty

Sour

Umami

Bitter

So almost all of the work you do to identify food flavors happens in your nose, through your sense of smell.

Our noses have **400** different receptors that can recognize up to **1 trillion** different odors, to help us identify the things we eat, and shouldn't eat, and everything that surrounds us all day long.

ODORS

1 trillion different odors! That's a lot. But scientists are discovering they fall into **10** different groups.

FRUITY

SICKENING & DECAYING

PUNGENT

CHEMICAL & SYNTHETIC

LEMONY

10

WOODY, MUSTY, & BURNT

FRAGRANT

MINTY

SWEET

TOASTY & NUTTY

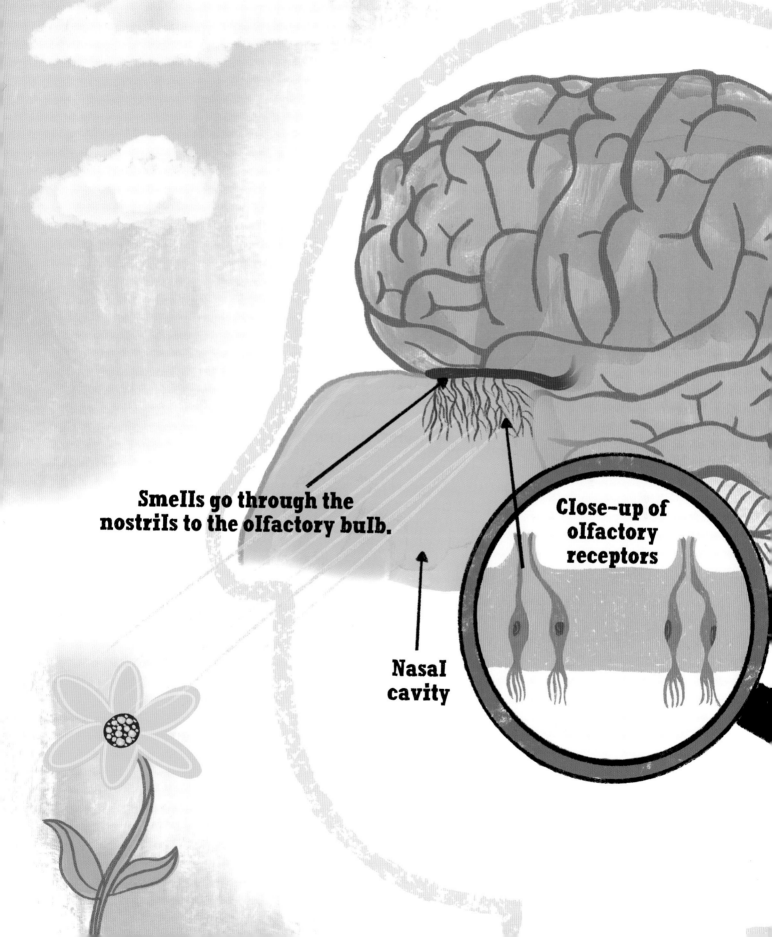

Smells go through the nostrils to the olfactory bulb.

Close-up of olfactory receptors

Nasal cavity

32 teeth
(MORE OR LESS)

Once you taste and smell your food, then you chew it

with your **32** teeth (more or less).

And swallow it.

Quite a lot of it, actually.

Around **1,500 pounds** per year.

In an average lifetime we eat somewhere around **55 tons** of it.

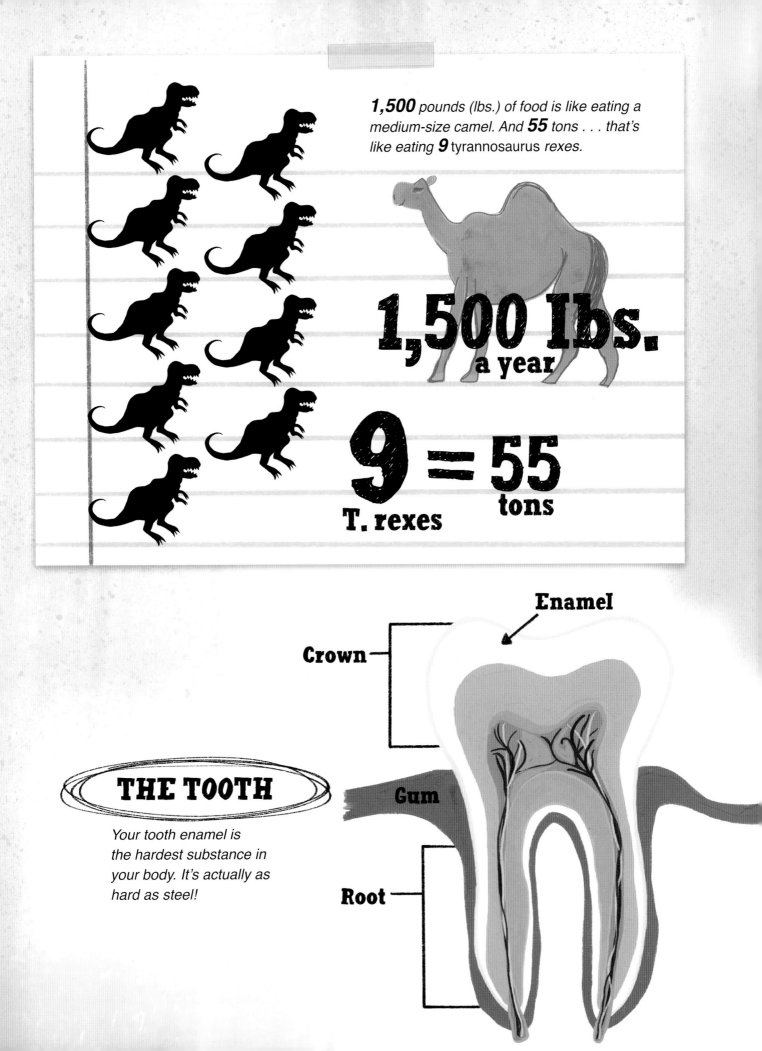

1,500 pounds (lbs.) of food is like eating a medium-size camel. And **55** tons . . . that's like eating **9** tyrannosaurus rexes.

1,500 lbs.
a year

9 = 55
T. rexes   tons

THE TOOTH

Your tooth enamel is the hardest substance in your body. It's actually as hard as steel!

Enamel

Crown

Gum

Root

And when you swallow,
the food goes down, down, down
into and through your stomach,
and through your intestines.

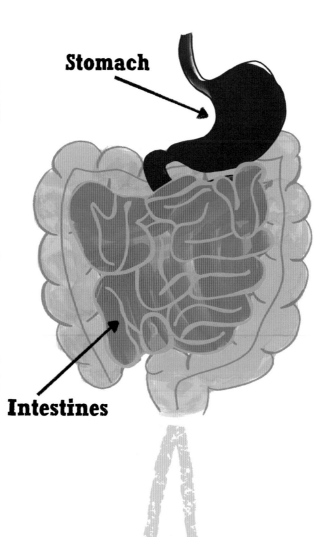

Stomach

Intestines

It takes about **10 seconds** for the food you chew to get to your stomach. It stays there for **3 to 4 hours**, getting broken down into a mush that moves into your intestines. Then it gets broken down even more, and the useful parts are sent to your bloodstream and to your cells—giving your body the energy it needs to keep you going. So the food you eat ends up feeding the cells that make you you. And the not-nutritious part that doesn't become you—well, that becomes poo!

From food to poo

Now intestines are something our bodies have quite a bit of.

Around **25 feet** of intestines.

That's as long as the height of a **2-story** house.

All curled up inside of you.

25 feet

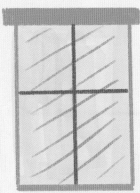

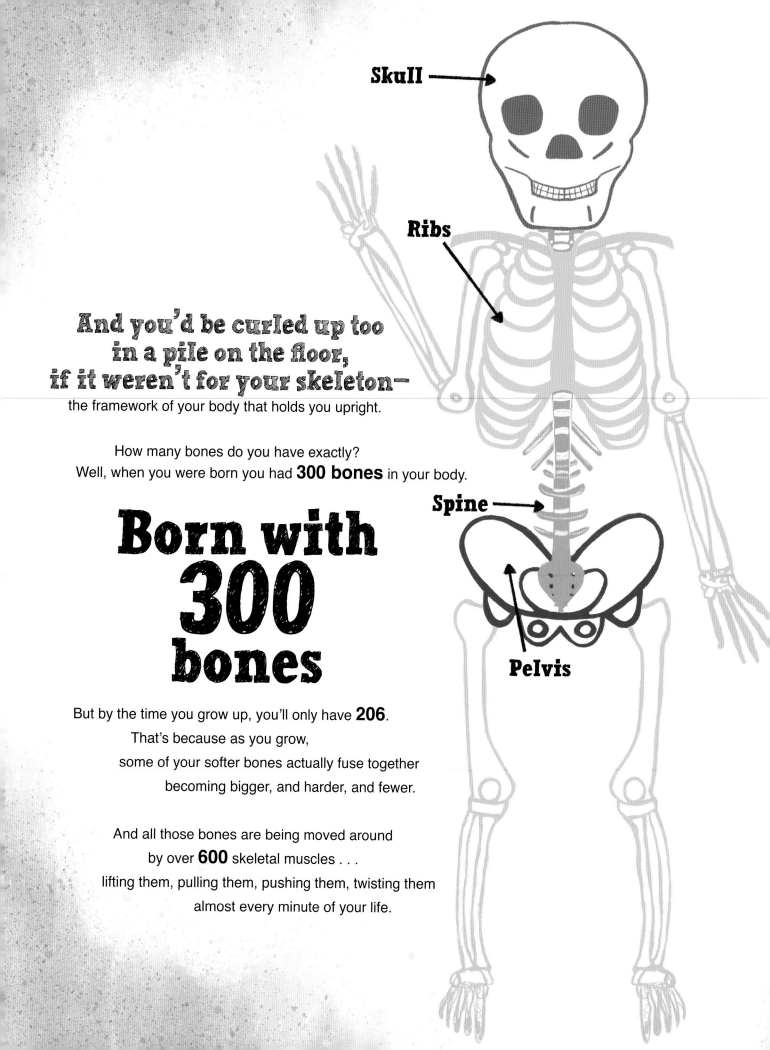

Skull

Ribs

Spine

Pelvis

And you'd be curled up too
in a pile on the floor,
if it weren't for your skeleton—
the framework of your body that holds you upright.

How many bones do you have exactly?
Well, when you were born you had **300 bones** in your body.

Born with 300 bones

But by the time you grow up, you'll only have **206**.
That's because as you grow,
some of your softer bones actually fuse together
becoming bigger, and harder, and fewer.

And all those bones are being moved around
by over **600** skeletal muscles . . .
lifting them, pulling them, pushing them, twisting them
almost every minute of your life.

The Leg

Bone

And, while your bones are holding you up,
gravity is pulling you down.
So much so that every night
you're about **⅓ of an inch** shorter than you were in the morning.
That's because all day long, gravity's pull
tugs on the soft cartilage between your bones
making you more and more compressed.

⅓ →

Kneecap

Cartilage

Bone

STRETCH!

Yes, gravity does shrink us during the day, while we're standing vertically. But don't worry! At night while we're horizontal, we stretch back out again.

Despite all that gravity, we do grow taller and grow up.

And, all the time you're growing, you're breathing, breathing, breathing . . .

20,000 breaths a day, **over 7 million** breaths a year.

120 GALLONS

To breathe we use our lungs. They are among the largest working parts of our body. And they work every minute of our lives, whether we're awake or asleep. Expanding to pull air in, and contracting to push breaths out. Every hour our lungs supply us with **120 gallons** *of the fresh new air we need to stay alive.*

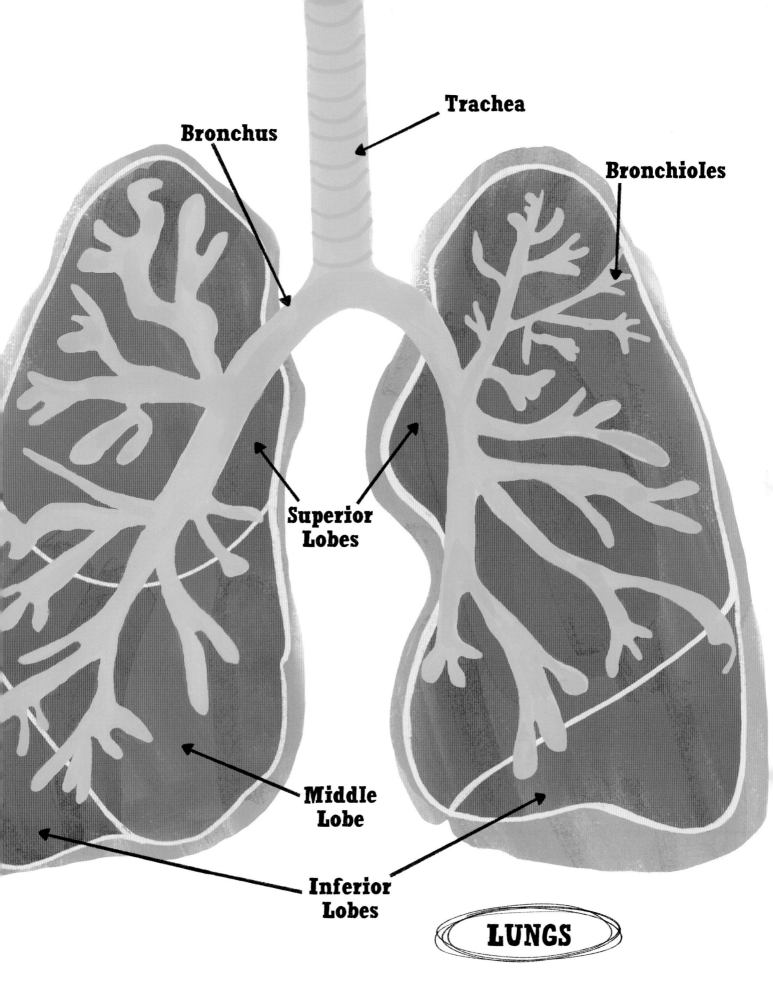

Trachea

Bronchus

Bronchioles

Superior
Lobes

Middle
Lobe

Inferior
Lobes

LUNGS

And while you're breathing and breathing,
your heart is beating, beating, beating.

Your little **10-ounce** heart
beats around **100,000** times a day . . .
That's **36 million** times per year.
All that heart beating pumps your blood round and round your body,
up to **3 times** a minute,
traveling through your blood vessels,
bringing oxygen and nutrients to every part of you.

Blood out of heart

Blood into heart

10-ounce heart

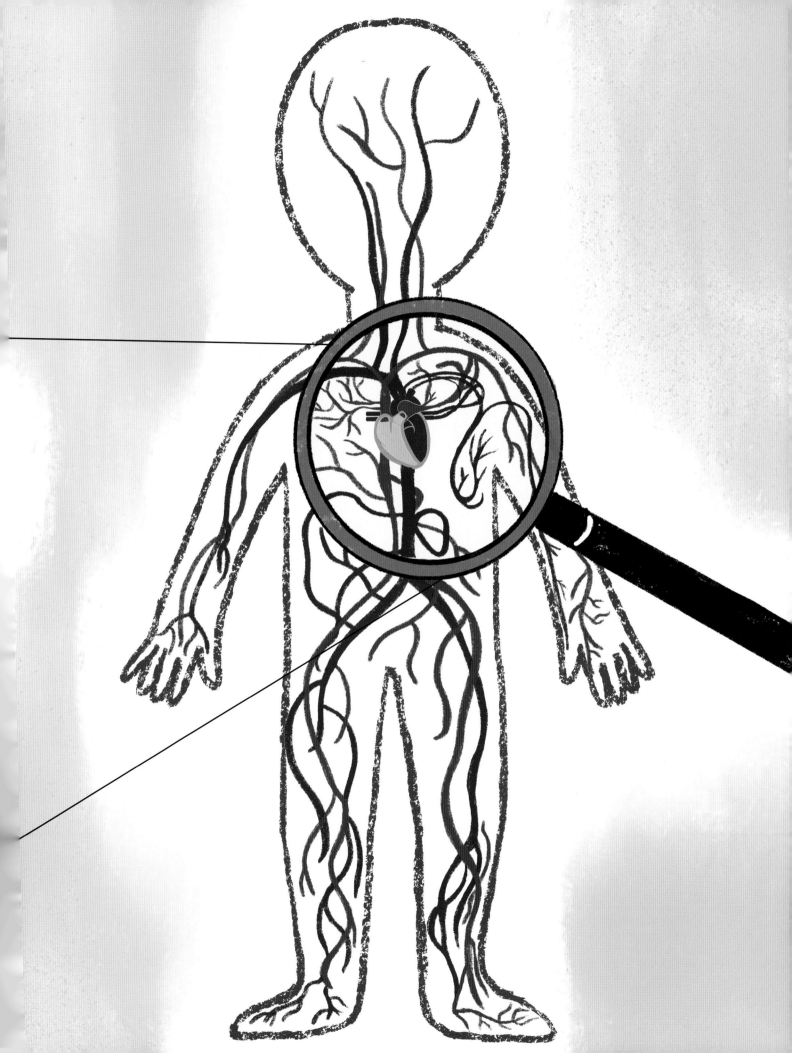

Your blood vessels are like little narrow tube-y threads all throughout your body.

And you've got lots and lots of them.
So many that if they were laid out end to end,
they would measure more than **60,000 miles** . . .
That's enough to circle the world . . . more than **twice**!

BLOOD VESSELS

Your body has **3 different kinds** of blood vessels: arteries, veins, and capillaries. The blood in your arteries flows away from your heart. The blood in your veins flows back to your heart. And your tiny little capillaries connect the two.

Artery   **Vein**

Capillaries

60,000 miles

Measured at its widest part—the equator—the Earth is **24,901 miles** around. That's huge. And yet, the length of your blood vessels is even huger. By a lot!

Speaking of the world, it's full of human bodies.

Can you guess how many?

Well, it's around **8 billion**.

8 billion fascinating amazing human bodies.

Our bodies . . . the link that connects us all.

The bond we all share.

The proof that we are **1 people**,

1 species, **1 family**.

Living together on planet Earth,

our **1 planet**, our **1 home**.

So the next time

someone mentions the human body to you

You can say,

"By the way, did you know . . ."

And share some amazing numbers

and fantastic facts with them.

8 BILLION
human
bodies

EVEN MORE FACTS ABOUT YOUR BODY

EVOLVING FACTS.
EVOLVING NUMBERS.

The facts and numbers you learn from this book, from other books, and in your classroom fall into two general categories: the ones that are settled and unchanging, and the ones that are evolving and changing. That's because of the way science works. Scientists are always searching, exploring, investigating, measuring, and discovering more and more until all the facts are known.

For instance, the number of bones in our bodies. That's settled science. It's known and it's not going to change. But the number of scents a human can smell, that's newer evolving science, still being researched. So that number will keep changing and becoming more precise over time, until scientists get the answers they're searching for.

And that shows us something wonderful about the human brain. It shows us that we're a curious species, always seeking to know, learn, and discover more.

BODY NUMBERS AND BODY PATTERNS

Our basic body numbers are ancient. The pattern of 2 eyes, 2 ears, 1 nose, 1 mouth, and 4 limbs is shared not only by apes, bears, cats, dogs, giraffes, mice, and frogs—but also by many dinosaurs (which first evolved 230 million years ago) and the even more ancient creatures that first crawled out of the ocean and onto land over 360 million years ago . . . .

CELLS

Every part of you is made of cells, from head to toe. Your 200 different kinds of cells are little factories that build you and keep you running—all working together to carry out your body's functions and keep you alive.

Your cells renew and repair your body, transport oxygen, fight infections, help you move, keep every one of your body parts functioning, give you energy, communicate with all the other cells in your body, and sense the world around you.

Most amazing, your cells are continually replacing themselves—at a rate of over 200 million per minute. Over and over throughout your entire life. So actually, you don't *have* cells, you *are* cells.

YOUR BRAIN

Your brain is the command center of all the actions and functions in your body—of everything you've read about in this book. It's where learning happens, thoughts, emotions, instincts, memories, your sense of humor, and creative ideas. All the special things that make you you.

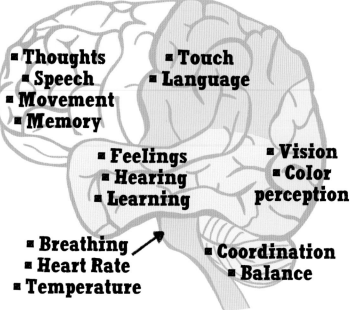

- **Thoughts**
- **Speech**
- **Movement**
- **Memory**
- **Touch**
- **Language**
- **Feelings**
- **Hearing**
- **Learning**
- **Vision**
- **Color perception**
- **Breathing**
- **Heart Rate**
- **Temperature**
- **Coordination**
- **Balance**

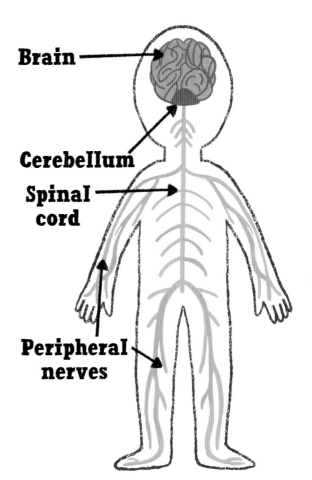

Brain

Cerebellum

Spinal cord

Peripheral nerves

It's where you connect to everything inside and out. In response to that input your brain makes decisions and sends trillions of electrical impulses through your nerves every second, telling your body what you want it to do.

To do all this, your brain's 86 billion cells use about 20 percent of your body's energy—more than any other organ in your body. And, although it's been compared to a computer, no computer can do the creative, inventive things our brains can do. For a little, wrinkly, gray mass of cells, about the size of two fists, your brain is definitely your prize possession. Your superpower.

YOUR NERVOUS SYSTEM

Your nervous system is your body's communication system. When you touch something, see something, hear something, feel something, how does your brain get the message? And how does your brain tell your body how to move, breathe, digest, react, think, function, and respond to everything inside and outside of you? It's all through the messages sent throughout your nervous system.

All those little electrical messages controlling your body travel to and from your brain, through your spinal column, and along your nerves—over 35 miles of nerves!—so you can do basically everything you do. Every second of your life.

So that makes your nervous system a pretty amazing system!

HUMAN BEINGS

Looking inside our bodies, scientists discovered that we are all virtually the same on the inside. That our skeletons, hearts, lungs, digestive systems, nerves, and our many body patterns

and parts prove we are all one species . . . *Homo sapiens*.

And that brings us to something else scientists know. That our species can be traced back to our original relatives. Our great-great-great- (you would have to say *great* thousands of times to get back that far) grandparents. And those great-grand relatives evolved at one prehistoric time, and one place on Earth.

The time was over two hundred thousand years ago. The place was in Africa. Archaeological finds prove it and our DNA (the little chemical packets inside our cells that tell us who is related to whom) proves it. All that science proves something amazing—that every single person who ever lived is related to every other one of us.

So here we are. One species. One people. One family. That's the spectacular fact that lives within our human bodies.

AUTHOR'S NOTE, SOURCES, AND RESOURCES

AUTHOR'S NOTE

From the time I was little, I have loved numbers. They could tell me how old I was, how tall I was, how far away a friend's house was, what a book cost, how long cookies had to stay in the oven and at what temperature, how fast a car was going, how high a building was and how deep the water was.

I noticed that streets had numbers, games had numbers, clocks and calendars had numbers, stories and songs had numbers. Numbers were everywhere.

Without numbers, things could be *big* or *small*, *fast* or *slow*, *heavy* or *light*, *young* or *old*—but numbers made them all precise, factual, and told the greater truth.

Numbers help us understand things and figure things out. They give us a powerful way to communicate. They are a fascinating language.

So now, after living a life filled with numbers, I'm happy to be writing a book—an entire series—in which numbers get to be my partner, my inspiration, and tool with which my collaborators and I get to tell our tales.

And what better tale to tell than the story of our very own amazing bodies!

LEARNING MORE ABOUT THE HUMAN BODY

If this book has made you curious to know more about your body and how it works, there are many fascinating ways to discover more about the bodies we all live in.

Ways to learn more, especially for kids:

BOOKS ABOUT OUR BODIES

Choi, Betty. *Human Body Learning Lab.* North Adams MA: Storey Publishing, 2022.

Thomas, Mindy and Raz, Guy. *Wow in the World: The How and Wow of the Human Body.* Boston: Houghton Mifflin Harcourt, 2021.

Walker, Richard. *Eyewitness: Human Body.* London: Dorling Kindersley, 2014.

WEBSITES

BrainPOPjr.: jr.brainpop.com/health/bodies

Human Body Learning: humanbodylearning.com

Nemours Kid's Health: kidshealth.org

EXHIBITS

You can find excellent exhibits and displays about the human body in natural history museums and science museums. Here are a few.

• Amazing Body Gallery, Health Museum, Houston TX

• Body Works, a touring exhibit, see schedule at bodyworks.com

• Human Body Gallery at the Science Museum of Minnesota, St. Paul MN

• World of Life at the California Science Center, Los Angeles CA

KITS, TOYS, MODELS, PUZZLES, AND POSTERS

There are many kits, toys, models, puzzles and posters based on the human body. Here are a few.

• Learning Resources Skeleton Floor Puzzle: a 4-foot-foam labeled skeleton puzzle.

• Learning Resources Anatomy Models: models of the heart, brain, body and skeleton.

• Palace Learning 3-Pack Anatomy Poster Set

• Palace Learning Brain Anatomy Poster

DOCUMENTARIES

There are documentaries about the body on TV, online, in the library, or available to rent. You can ask your teachers or school librarians to help you find these, or use this website: topdocumentaryfilms.com/human-body/.

NEWS ON TV, IN NEWSPAPERS, AND MAGAZINES

Because there is so much scientific research being done on the body, there are often new and fascinating discoveries that these researchers are coming up with. And sometimes these new discoveries are reported in newspapers, magazines or even on TV. So ask your family members and teachers to tell you when one of these interesting new discoveries appears in the news. Perhaps you could start a scrapbook of them.

SOURCES AND RESOURCES USED TO CREATE THIS BOOK

Books

Bryson, Bill. *The Body: A Guide for Occupants.* New York: Anchor Books, 2021.

DK. *How the Body Works: The Facts Simply Explained.* New York: Dorling Kindersley, 2016.

DK. *Human Body: A Visual Encyclopedia,* 2nd edition. New York: Dorling Kindersley, 2018.

DK Smithsonian. *Knowledge Encyclopedia: Human Body!* New York: Dorling Kindersley, 2017.

Page, Martyn. *Human Body: An Illustrated Guide to Every Part of the Human Body and How it Works.* New York: Dorling Kindersley, 2001.

Roberts, Alice. *The Complete Human Body: The Definitive Visual Guide,* 2nd edition. New York: Dorling Kindersley, 2016

Websites

Arizona State University: askabiologist.asu.edu

Inner Body: innerbody.com

Live Science: livescience.com

Medical News Today: medicalnewstoday.com

WebMd: webmd.com

COUNTING ON **YOUR** BODY

HOW MUCH BLOOD DO YOU HAVE?

Not everyone has the same amount of blood.

It depends on a person's size and age. So how much do YOU have?

You can look at the chart below and figure it out.

Newborn	40 pounds	60 pounds	80 pounds	100 pounds	120 pounds	Adult females	Adult males
1 CUP	5–6 CUPS	7–8 CUPS	10–11 CUPS	14–15 CUPS	16–17 CUPS	18–20 CUPS	23–25 CUPS

If your weight is in-between these examples, estimate how much blood you have. For instance, someone who weighs 90 pounds has around 12-13 cups of blood.

HOW FAST DOES *YOUR* HEART BEAT?

You can find out how fast your heart is beating by measuring your "pulse." Your "pulse rate" is the number of times your heart beats in 1 minute.

To take your pulse, put 2 fingers of your hand near the thumb-side of your other wrist. Press very gently and you will feel the beat-beat-beat of your blood flowing through your artery. Count those beats for 1 minute. (Someone else can tell you when the minute starts and stops.) The number of beats you count is your pulse, also called your "heart rate."

Take your pulse when you're resting, then try it again after you've run and jumped around for about a minute. See how much faster your heart beats after you've been active.

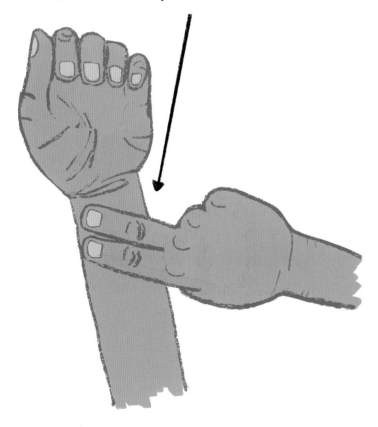

COUNTING *YOUR* BONES

How many bones do you have in your hand?

Look at your hand and count how many bones you have in your fingers. Next, guess how many bones there are in the rest of your hand.

Now look at the diagram of all the bones in a hand. Count the bones and see how close your guess was.

MEASURING **YOUR** PROPORTIONS

The "proportions" of your body is the measurement of one body part compared to another. To measure YOUR body's proportions you can use pieces of string or yarn to measure each body part, and then see how it compares to another.

Try these and see what results you get.

1 Compare your height to the width of your arm span (from left fingertip to right fingertip). In most people it's the same.

2 Compare the length of your face to the length of your hand. Are they the same? They usually are.

3 Now measure the length of your foot and compare it to your forearm (from the inside of your elbow to your wrist). The same again? Usually yes.

4 Measure your femur, the bone that goes from your hip to your knee. Now measure your height. Your height is probably 4 times as long as your femur.